The Art of Forgiveness

GEORGE ARKHURST

Published by Gloripub
Printed in the U.S.A
Copyright © 2018 George Arkhurst
All rights reserved solely by the author. The author guarantees all contents are original and do not infringe upon legal rights of any other person or work. No part of this book may be reproduced in any form except for brief quotations in printed reviews, without the permission of the author.

Unless otherwise indicated, the Bible quotations are taken from the from the King James Bible.
.

Request for information should be addressed to:

ISBN-13: 978-0997621372
ISBN-10: 0997621370

Contents

Dedication   i

Acknowledgments   iii

Preface   vii

One   1

What is Forgiveness? 1

Two   15

Three.   34

Struggling with Forgiveness   34

Four 63

The Practicality of Forgiving Others. 63

Living with the offender after forgiveness.   87

****

Dedication

****

This book is dedicated to my beloved darling wife, Fatmata and my awesome children, Fanta, Cassandra, Sade and George Jr.

****

Acknowledgments

****

God Almighty who had done marvelously well in guiding me through life's path and the writing of another book. My parents: the late Mr. Jerry Kwesi Arkhurst and Mrs. Cassandra Arkhurst. My Pastor, Benjamin Boakye, head pastor of Ebenezer Assembly of God church, Bronx, NY; for his support and his willingness to help me greatly in ministry. My wife who has been the voice of reasoning, making sure the best of me is given to my work. My daughter Fanta, who helped with proofreading and editing. My able boss and Sunday School superintendent, Minister James Mensah, for his relentless support, editing and brainstorming. My brother, my friend the one and only Minister Tony Aghamiogie, who is always willing to give helping hand in editing and ratings. My Bro, General Eric Asiedu, who is a part of the trio in original editing. Minister Alphina ByFaith Dumbuya of the morning crew International Ministry, whose message of "forgetting the past" that I listened to one morning, inspired a part of this book. A teacher, I met in the Metro North train, who edited a portion of the manuscript during a trip from Grand Central Station to Stamford. My friends, Francis Lemeh and Clarence Cole who were visiting from London for holidays but had time to help with proofreading and editing. Francis did spend a considerable time proofreading and editing a good portion of this book. My friend Que La who willingly saw the need to edit and did so to a portion of the book; My sister, my friend, Joyce Agyemang for her gentle reminder and encouragement to write, and John Rutere who is an inspiration and motivator in both of my publications. My sister Matilda Sarkodie who recently became my number one fan, sharing my posts on face book. Finally, to every single one of my brothers and sisters in Christ, and to all my friends and well-wishers, I say a big thank you and God richly bless you all.

****

Preface

****

"For if you forgive other people when they sin against you, your heavenly Father will also forgive you. ¹⁵ But if you do not forgive others their sins, your Father will not forgive your sins." Mathew 6:14-15

Forgiveness is one of the most challenging aspects of life that man must address. Man must forgive his fellow man or risks the forgiveness of God. In a world where wickedness is the order of the day. Where hatred and its by-products are produced and carried out by the minute, a world where people suffer in the hands of others, it is evident that in such society we will hurt each other, and sometimes very badly. Man had been wicked to his fellow man as early back as at creation and this has permeated societies and communities and has extended to the whole world.

Some of these acts of men are so atrocious; they cause one to flinch. People plan things that are so wicked; it is hard to imagine it until it is carried out. Yet such people must be forgiven. How do you forgive someone who knowingly and deliberately inflicts injuries on you? Someone who rapes, someone who defraud people of their hard-earned cash, causing them to lose their homes? Someone who kills others indiscriminately? How can survivors of those murdered forgive the murderers? Where can one muster the courage to forgive those who prey on children sexually? Yet, if one does not forgive the other that wronged him, regardless of how gruesome the offenses might be, risks God's forgiveness.

Forgiveness is a very complicated thing to grasp. It is hard to understand why God who is good, able and just; not only seemingly allow these inhumane things to happen. But is asking or commanding that the perpetrators be forgiven? How can anyone be able to forgive? This book intends to do an expository on the topic of forgiveness, so people can get a better understanding and benefits from the blessings that come with it.

x

****

One

What is Forgiveness?

****

A Process

Forgiveness is the process by which one intentionally stops resenting or harboring hatred and grudges for someone that had hurt them. It is the careful consideration of the pros and cons of its effects and benefits. It is that which when acted upon rightly, brings peace, joy, and reconciliation. It builds up relationships that had once been broken, which in turn, brings peace to individuals and communities. However, when acted upon wrongly, it becomes a brooding ground for all types of maliciousness, bitterness, anger and hatred. Generally, people want to live happy and peaceful lives, but the one thing that stands in their way is their inability to forgive.

To forgive people when they wrong you is not the first thing that comes to your mind. On the contrary, you will want to revenge if you can, and if you can't, you become bitter and resentful toward the offender. Until you are faced with a situation where you have been gravely wronged, you might not understand the full gravity of forgiveness.

I have heard stories of hurting people, people that had been scarred from what others had done to them. Such people do not have the intention to forgive their offenders. They carry deep-seated resentments in their hearts, which can occupy and dominate their thoughts and can propel them in the wrong direction in life.

Unforgiveness is deadly. It eats people up like cancer and alters people's destiny most of the time. It is a hard way to live, but very many people are living their lives like that, and it seems there is no getting away from it. The good news is, you don't have to live like that anymore.

There is a way to overcome unforgiveness and live a happy and productive life. God had provided a method by which every one of us should be able to forgive the wrongs done to us. He took the initiative to forgive our sins first. Scripture says, *"But God demonstrates his own love for us in this: While we were still sinners, Christ died for us. Romans 5:8*

God's intentions are for us to be forgiven and to have the ability to forgive others. God literally had Christ died for us! Demonstrating His ability to forgive. Question is why? Because of the Love He has for man.

What Motivates Forgiveness?

In societies across the world, there have always been instances where love is bestowed on someone that is seemingly undeserving of it. Like a husband making excuses for his wife's bad behavior toward him. Like a son who is a menace to society but has a mother who loves and protects him. Even though the husband and the mother are aware of how badly they are being treated by wife and son respectively, the love they have for them excuses it all. They will try everything in their power to change their behaviors because of love. Love is what causes people to do things that they will not do under normal circumstances. It is that which alters behaviors in given situations. When we read the accounts of God's love for man in the Bible it is not far-fetched from the actions described above.

God loves mankind. His love is seen in all that he had done and is still doing for man. God was not the one who broke the relationship that existed at creation. He did everything good for man, but man repaid by disobeying him. That disobedience brought about sin and hostility to the whole human race and that severed the bond between God and man. But because of his love for us, he reached out and forgave our sins. God's love for man is amazing. His love motivates him to send his Son to pay the price we ought to pay. *"For God so love the world that He gave His only begotten Son, that whosoever believes in Him shall not perish but have eternal life"* Jn. 3:16

When I ponder the love that God has for humans, I picture it like a very wealthy and influential man who had a family he really cherished. And because he cherished them, he did everything in his ability to make them very happy and lived exquisite lives. This man purchased a massive piece of land and built an estate that surpasses everything ever constructed before and after his lifetime. He had the finest houses with beautiful decors. His landscaping was out of this world. He had the finest cars, trucks, planes and every luxurious thing one can imagine. He had a variety of businesses, factories etc. This man eventually got married and had kids. He built theme parks, game rooms, arcades and everything that made the kids happy. Kids were sent to the best schools. While other kids took buses and trains to school, his kids were driven in limousines and when they were old enough to drive, they all had their cars. Everything for them was state of the art. From the types of cars they drove to the gadgets they owned. They were the envy of all the kids and even adults in their neighborhood.

One fine evening at dinner, their father asked them to do one thing for him, he asked them to get serious in school so that they will continue his legacy. This wealthy and influential man had provided his family with everything. They had the best doctors, dentists and so on. They had lots and lots of money in their names in banks all over their city. What a fine life?

These kids heard what their father had asked of them. They endeavored to keep it that way for a while, but somewhere down the road, they got mixed up with the wrong crowds. They started going away from their dad's request. They hung out late, partying almost all the time. Grades were dropping, and they slowly got into drugs and alcohol. They got so bad; their father had to kick them out. They spiraled downward, hit rock bottom and turned to crime. Eventually, the law caught up with them. They were tried and found guilty. At their sentencing, the court was packed full. It was a spectacle because of their reputation. These were the rich man's kids! Amongst the people in the courthouse that day, was one unexpected guest. The court was called to session, the Judge took his seat and called for the accused. As they were marching them to the witness stand, they saw their father sitting in the front row. Their hearts dropped. They felt embarrassed and very uneasy. Their father had loved them and had lavished on them so much. They could have obeyed and pleased him if anything, but they followed their hearts and desires. Now in front of all these people, they had put their father to shame. They could not hold his gaze as he studied them one by one. Court was in full session, and the judge read their sentences. They were guilty and will do many years in Jail. As they were about to be whisked away, something strange happened. Their father stood up and asked the judge if he could ask for one thing? His children became frightened. What was he going to say; but to let them feel the brunt of their foolishness. He was furious at them and will address them in that tone before they get carried away. However, they

The Art of Forgiveness

were shocked and amazed when they heard their father asked the judge if he could go to jail for his children. The rich man's love for his children motivated him to take their punishment and forgave their wrongs.

This illustration is the closest I can come to put visual effects in the way God loves us, humans.

What's the Basis of Forgiveness?

For forgiveness to take effect, there must be an offense. A crime committed, a debt owed or a wrong done. Someone would have to have wronged someone else to warrant forgiveness. When it comes to God, man has always wronged him. Referencing my story above, the basis for which the father took the punishment was because of his children's crimes. If they had lived obediently to their father, there would have been no reason for their father to take their punishment. In the same vein, we understand that sin is the basis of God's forgiveness to man. If there had been no sin, there would have been no need for Jesus to die. We will all be living peaceful and sinless lives. But on the contrary, we are living in a troubled world. An imperfect and sinful world. A world which had deviated from its original state. The Bible taught us that God created this beautiful Earth. At the end of all his creation, God made man. The scriptures tell us that God called out everything, and they came to be; but when it came to mankind, it was announced or declared, *"Let us make mankind in Our Image, in Our Likeness, so that they may rule…" Genesis 1:26.* The Bible says God formed man from the dust of the earth and then he breathed the breath of life into man's nostrils. Man is indeed God's prized possession! At the end of it all, God looked upon his creation and saw that it was very good.

"In the beginning God created the heaven and the earth…³¹ And God saw everything that he had made, and, behold, it was very good. And the evening and the morning were the sixth day." Genesis 1:1; 31

God introduced man to the vast world he had created for him. He gave him authority to rule and govern over all the works of his hands. Adam, the man God created became the sole owner of the entire world. He was the wealthiest man on earth and lived a very prosperous life. Everything was given to him. Like the kids in my story, Adam lived a life of luxury. He owned and oversaw everything.

At some point during their interaction, God gave him a command, just one simple command. *"And the LORD God commanded the man, you are free to eat from any tree in the garden, but you must not eat from the tree of the knowledge of good and evil…" Genesis 2:16-17.* Continuing the creation account, it is recorded that man ate of the tree that God had warned him not to eat from. Because of that one act of disobedience, sin entered the world. And sin produces, bitterness, envy, jealousy, hatred and every inconceivable wickedness in the heart of man. These became recipes and convenient reservoirs to harbor grievances and unforgiveness.

Shortly after that disobedient act of Adam, it's effect caught up with him. Not only was he driven out of the garden which was home to him, but his firstborn killed his younger brother. Ever since that time, man had been on the path of destruction. Humankind had engaged in a systematic way to destroy each other. The venom of sin is deeply entrenched within the heart of man. God saw his prized possession; his masterpiece embarked on a path of destruction. On a path of unbearable repercussions. Man to man, doing wicked things to each other.

In our world today, man's hatred for each other is on the increase. You see bigotry and nepotism, racism and tribalism. Men fighting each other, killing, maiming, and doing whatever wicked act there is. People are killing others and selling their body parts. People are enslaving their fellow humans for their selfish gains. This attitude of hate and selfishness that humanity had cultivated is displeasing to God. The Bible records and reveals the way God felt seeing man's wickedness toward his fellow man.

"And GOD saw that the wickedness of man was great in the earth, and that every

imagination of the thoughts of his heart was only evil continually. And it repented the LORD that he had made man on the earth, and it grieved him at his heart." Genesis 6:5-6.

No father on earth loves to see his children fighting each other, let alone fighting to destruction. God doesn't like it when we fight; he would love to see us loving each other. Every time, any of us hurt the next person, we are sinning against God because that person is God's prized possession. It was based on this growing wickedness that seemingly knows no bounds that God's forgiveness is called into play.

The Cost of Forgiveness.

Forgiveness is costly. It is not something that God did because he is God and can just forgive people's sins. He paid for it. It took God's dearest and best to pay the price for our sins, paving the way for forgiveness. Most, if not all the time, we do not see the emotional side of God. We accept the things he does without realizing what it takes from his point of view. We let our knowledge or imagination of his ability overshadows that part of him. Sending his Son to earth must have left emotions on him. It was not easy for him to have watched his Son being ill-treated. It was not easy for him to have watched him being killed horribly.

Our forgiveness not only cost God this much emotionally, but it also cost Jesus his life! He was killed like a common criminal, a shameful and disgraceful death to accomplish the standard by which man will forever be forgiven. Let's ponder and play this over in our minds for a second. Which of us will let our son die in the place of another person. Especially if that person had wronged us.

Before Jesus came down to earth and die, the Bible tells us that Jesus was with God at creation. And that all things were made by him. *"All things were made by Him and without Him was not anything made that was made" John 1:3.* Jesus was there creating the universe with God, but he had to come down to earth for man's forgiveness. He emptied himself of his reputation. The Bible says:

> "... *Christ Jesus, Who, being in very nature[a] God, did not consider equality with God something to be used to his own advantage;* ⁷ *rather, he made himself nothing by taking the very nature[b] of a servant, being made in human likeness.* ⁸ *And being found in appearance as a man, he humbled himself by becoming obedient to death— even death on a cross! Philippians 2:5-8.*

Jesus emptied himself of what he is known to be just to die for us, that was selfless and costly!

We see how much of a sacrifice God made and how Jesus gave the ultimate sacrifice in a bid to establish forgiveness. In the light of this much sacrifice as we have read, how much are we willing to sacrifice to further the course of forgiveness. Forgiving all that will sin against you and as many times as they will do so. *"Even if they sin against you seven times in a day and seven times come back to you saying 'I repent,' you must forgive them." Lk. 17:3.* Will you do it?

****

Two

Jesus Taught Forgiveness.

****

Passively

On many occasions, Jesus taught people in clear and practical terms. He used examples that people can relate to and that can be easily understood. When he taught forgiveness, he did so passively and actively.

To impart the 'know-how' of how to forgive, Jesus chose twelve men, with whom he worked closely. Those men, except for the one who later betrayed him, were with him throughout his ministry, and were witnesses to all the controversies he faced. They observed the many confrontations and conflicts he had with the Jewish religious leaders. They witnessed the plot against him. They saw when Judas betrayed and got him arrested. They saw when he was led away to the High Priest, then to Pilate and then to Herod. They saw him been sentenced to death by Pilate. They witnessed Him underneath the wooden cross; they were there when the crown of thorns was thrust on his head. They saw when he was flogged thirty-nine times. Each stripe tore his skin.

Those men were witnesses when they laid our Lord Jesus on the cross, put his feet together and put a huge nail to it and hammered through. They saw his arms stretched out to the right and the left and nailed. Every single stroke left a sound in their hearts. They saw men making a mockery of him. They were present when the cross was picked up. They looked at him; they saw when his side was pierced with a spear. Those men must have been bewildered beyond imagination.

As they were trying to process these acts of injustice, as they were trying to console and comfort each other and possibly thinking of what to do next; they heard

Jesus said: - *"Father, forgive them, for they do not know what they are doing." Luke 23:34.* Those words uttered by Jesus, I am sure left them totally perplexed. How can such wickedness be forgiven? They can't possibly fathom that. However, those men witnessed the art of forgiveness first hand. They saw God demonstrating his love through forgiveness for mankind, setting an example of how the world should cultivate that attitude. Those men saw how Jesus reacted in every giving circumstance and made mental notes of those actions.

Knowing the World Enhances Forgiveness

Jesus ability to forgive and to teach men how to do so comes from his knowledge of the world. He knew how the world operates. He knew that this world is full of wickedness and that the progression of it will be on the increase throughout the ages. He knew firsthand what it felt like to be subjected to inhumane treatments. He experienced the pains, anxieties, betrayals and all the adverse effect of man's cruelty. He endured them all because he was prepared and ready to deal with them. Jesus' knowledge of how this world operates prepared him to deal with every aspect of life here on earth. One of which was dealing with the wickedness done to him by mankind.

He never held grudges, nor was he disgruntled, or felt anxious and had anxieties. Even though, he was often buffeted and lived under the same circumstances as we do, he triumphed over all the adverse things that were thrown at him. These are the very same things that bothers and defeats us. None of the bitter experiences he had, deprived him of living a peaceful life. He lived a conscious, peaceful and exemplary life, knowing fully well that his disciples were learning from him. His was and still is a life worth copying.

Actively

Forgiveness is so complex, that the passive teachings of Jesus alone did not cover the topic in detail. In a well-narrated parable, Jesus explained the consequences man faces if he fails to forgive his fellow man. He did so when he answered a question Peter had posed to him. Capitalizing on that question, he taught on the conditionality of forgiveness, portraying it to be the most critical.

Peter was one of Jesus' disciples, who first heard about forgiving others when the Lord taught them to pray in what we know as the Lord's Prayer.

And forgive us our debts, as we forgive our debtors. And lead us not into temptation, but deliver us from evil: For thine is the kingdom, and the power, and the glory, forever. Amen.

For if ye forgive men their trespasses, your heavenly Father will also forgive you: But if ye forgive not men their trespasses, neither will your Father forgive your trespasses. Mathew 6:12-15

Peter, who grew up under the law and was familiar with the "an eye for an eye" teachings, seemed to have a hard time understanding forgiveness. After all, paying someone back for what they did to you seems justifiable. I believed the words

"For if ye forgive men their trespasses, your heavenly Father will also forgive you: [15] But if ye forgive not men their trespasses, neither will your Father forgive your trespasses" Mathew 12:14-15 played on his mind constantly. Trying to make sense of it, he came to Jesus and asked:-

"Then Peter came to Jesus and asked, "Lord, how many times shall I forgive my brother or sister who sins against me? Up to seven times?" Mather 18:21.

Peter's question was indicative that he would have loved to repay someone who had hurt him. His question to the Lord echoed a cry for a better understanding of what forgiving others really means. Peter wanted to know if at some point, it is okay revenge on someone who had hurt him more than seven times. That question prompted Jesus to give a more detailed, all in all, teaching about forgiveness.

> *"Therefore is the kingdom of heaven likened unto a certain king, which would take account of his servants. And when*

he had begun to reckon, one was brought unto him, which owed him ten thousand talents. But forasmuch as he had not to pay, his lord commanded him to be sold, and his wife, and children, and all that he had, and payment to be made. The servant therefore fell down, and worshipped him, saying, Lord, have patience with me, and I will pay thee all. Then the lord of that servant was moved with compassion, and loosed him, and forgave him the debt. But the same servant went out, and found one of his fellow servants, which owed him an hundred pence: and he laid hands on him, and took him by the throat, saying, Pay me that thou owest. And his fellow servant fell down at his feet, and besought him, saying, Have patience with me, and I will pay thee all. And he would not: but went and cast him into prison, till he should pay the debt. So when his fellow servants saw what was done, they were very sorry, and came and told unto their lord all that was done. Then his lord, after that he had called him, said unto him, O thou wicked servant, I forgave thee all that debt, because thou desiredst me: Shouldest not thou also have had compassion on thy fellow servant, even as I had pity on *thee? And his lord was worth, and delivered him to the tormentors, till he should pay all that was due unto him. So likewise shall my heavenly Father do also unto you, if ye from your hearts forgive not everyone his brother their trespasses."* Mathew 18:23-35

This narrative had always focused on the wicked servant's attitude and subsequent punishment that stemmed from it. But it teaches a lesson far deeper than that. It depicts the way the world reacts when it comes to forgiveness and how it will eventually play out.

As always, Jesus used earthly things to teach heavenly truths. In this teaching, he drew an inference from a King. He presented a scenery where a King sat on his throne and summoned all his debtors. It was the day of reckoning. He wanted to get his money back from all who owed him. At some point during his reign, it seems people had reached out to him for monetary help. The king may have drawn up contracts to ensure he gets paid back at a set time. He had books of records where he wrote down every debt owed to him. And the day he had set aside came and he was reckoning with his debtors.

The lesson portrayed in this section of the parable teaches that, like the king, God has set a day aside to reckon with the world. He has books in which he records all our actions and that one day, there will be a reckoning. Scriptures says:-

> *Then I saw a great white throne and him who was seated on it. The earth and the heavens fled from his presence, and there was no place for them. And I saw the dead, great and small, standing before the throne, and books were opened. Another book was opened, which is the book of life. The dead were judged according to what they had done as recorded in the books."* Revelation 20:11-12

On that day, all will be gathered in front of God's throne. The Bible say the books will be opened. Someone's name will be called, and commendations of that person will be read. It will be something in the likes of Jesus's visitation to the Churches back in the days. I know your works, how well, you preached, or how well you taught. How you stood firm and did not compromise with unbelievers. I know how you fasted and prayed every Friday night. Your dedication to preparing and teaching Bible truths. I know how you worship me early in the morning, how you sing well in the choir. How you constantly called and follow up on people. I know how you took your clothes off your back and gave it to someone that indeed needed it most. I commend you for all those things, but! Wait a minute, there is a but, and where there is a but, it means a change of direction.

Imagine, that is you for a second, you are standing in front of God Almighty. Your heart is pounding, probably sweating waiting for the next words out of the Lord's mouth. The Lord looks you straight in the eyes, probably shaking his head from left to right. Feeling the pain of what is about to happen to you. The Lord our God is compassionate. I can imagine his compassion kicking in even at this point as he holds your gaze. The unfortunate thing is he cannot do anything to save you at that time. He will not be the one judging you. He said the words that we all have heard will be the judge on that day. *There is a judge for the one who rejects me and does not accept my words; the very words I have spoken will condemn them at the last day." John 12:48*

He will not be condemning you, the words you've said over and over, like the words in the Lord's prayer that you have said repeatedly over time, will be the judge. In the words of that prayer, you have said "*…forgive us our sins, as we forgive those who sin against us. …Mathew 6:12.*" This is the only prayer that you are staking your life on. You are asking God to forgive you only when you forgive your fellow man. And you have failed to do so.

Reading from the open books, the Lord continues from where he left off. He says, but I have this one thing against you, you did not forgive your brother when he sinned against you! Imagine that for a second. There is no turning back then. Will it be worth it?

What happens next in the parable is the pivotal lesson the Lord intends to put across. A servant was found who owed a considerable amount of money to the King. He was called and asked to pay, and because he could not pay, the King ordered him punished. It happened that the servant pleaded with the King and was forgiven. The King pitied him, and he let him go free of every penny he owed.

After he left the King's presence, he ran into a coworker, who owed him a fraction of what he owed the King. He demanded to be paid, but his colleague did not have the money to pay and pleaded with him. He did not listen to the pleas of his coworker but threw him in Jail. The King got wind of what he had done and became angry at him. He summoned that wicked servant to his presence, reinstated the debt he owed all over again, and ask him to pay. Because the servant could not pay, the King send him to jail till he can pay.

There are in-depth lessons taught in this parable that can easily be missed. The servant in the story failed to see them and is being used as a lesson, to teach us not make the same mistakes he made. The servant was not mindful of these few things in the parable that I have listed below.

I. He was not mindful of the magnitude of the debt he owed.

The servant owed the King a huge sum of money which he forgot about after he had received the King's pardon. The king had to remind him of the magnitude of his debt that he forgave as compared to what his colleague owed him. The servant did not consider that when he demanded payment from his colleague.

In this part of the parable, Jesus intends for us to consider the magnitude of our sins as compared to the sins others commit against us. If we can take an inventory of how great a forgiveness we have received from God, it will motivate us to develop a forgiving spirit. Because the sins we commit against God far outnumbers the sins anyone can commit against us.

II. He was not mindful of the precedence the King established.

It seemed the King had established forgiveness as a practice in his kingdom. He forgave the wicked servant as a precedence and was expecting the servant to do the same in keeping with that precedence. The lesson here is, like the King, God had set a precedence in this world by forgiving our sins. His desire is for man to forgive his fellow man as he had done for us. He initiated forgiveness and kept it active in so much that he sent his son to pay the price for our sins. God intends to have people live in peace, free of debt from him and each other.

III. This servant was not mindful of whom he owed. He owed the King who is the one single authority of that kingdom.

The servant was not cognizant of the fact that the King is the sole authority of the land. And that to be in debt to him was not the smartest idea. He should have known that the King can make decisions as he sees fit, and that he is not answerable to anyone.

It would have been worth the while if the servant had recognized what the King did when he forgave him and had led a quiet life after that. He took matters into his own hands sending his coworker to jail. The king had no choice but to assert his authority and punished the wicked servant.

This part of the parable is speaking of God's authority in plain terms. God is the sole and absolute authority of this universe and it should be noteworthy for us to realize that. When we sin, we sin against the single most powerful authority in the world and if he chose to pardon our sins, we should be wise enough to do likewise.

Like the wicked servant in the parable, very many of us have failed in the three areas discussed above. We are not mindful of them at all and are likely to err, like he did. We are not willing to let go of the wrongs of others. We seek to pay them back. We are not mindful of the fact that God who is the highest authority, forgave us for us to forgive others, in keeping with his policy.

In conclusion Jesus warned that God would do exactly what the King did to the wicked servant. He would not forgive the sins of anyone who does not forgive his fellow man. If God does not forgive, it means one thing, you will have to pay. Will it be worth losing God's forgiveness over some bad things someone did to you? Would you let yourself fall into the servant's error and pay the utmost price?

At the end of the teachings, I believe Peter began to understand the art of forgiveness. He began to see the bigger picture. The reality that God forgave his many sins hit him. He realized that if God can forgive him that many sins, he should be able to forgive his fellow man. Peter began to understand that every man is valuable in God's eyes. He began to understand that God really loves mankind, so he stirred up himself to forgive all who had offended him. However, Peter's determination to forgive people does not mean he got the know-how or the skills to do so just yet. He still needs the Master's guidelines just as we all do.

Learning from Jesus.

Jesus understood Peter's position, he knew Peter, like many of us don't have a clue on how to even start to forgive people. You might have had some wicked things done to you. Things you find very hard to even think of forgiving. And now you are reading that God will not forgive you if you do not forgive that person. You find yourself in a real struggle, you want to do right, but finding it extremely difficult.

Jesus saw that in you and in me and in everyone else. He saw our struggles in this area, and he responded admonishing us to do this: - *"Take my yoke upon you and learn from me, for I am gentle and humble in heart, and you will find rest for your souls."* Mathew 11:29.

To learn from someone will mean to have seen the person teach either actively or passively. Jesus lived an exemplary life, purposely teaching all around him who were willing to learn. In his days on earth, religion was the order of the day, and people took interest in how people lived their lives. Both his followers and critics knew Jesus was different. His life stood out from the rest of them, he lived by certain rules that no one understood. The twelve men he chose observed his way of life and were always in awe of him, at one point they asked themselves, "...*what kind of man is this...*" *Mathew 8:27*. On every instant they noted how he conducted himself.

Jesus knew he had made indelible marks on his follower, and that made it easier for him to pass on the rules by which he had lived. At a close session with his disciples he gave a series of instructions on how to entreat people when they are offended.

"But I say unto you, that ye resist not evil: but whosoever shall smite thee on thy right cheek, turn to him the other also. [40] And if any man will sue thee at the law, and take away thy coat, let him have thy cloak also. [41] And whosoever shall compel thee to go a mile, go with him twain. [42] Give to him that asketh thee, and from him that would borrow of thee turn not thou away. [43] Ye have heard that it hath been said, Thou shalt love thy neighbour, and hate thine enemy. [44] But I say unto you, Love your enemies, bless them that curse you,

do good to them that hate you, and pray for them which despitefully use you, and persecute you;[45] *That ye may be the children of your Father which is in heaven: for he maketh his sun to rise on the evil and on the good, and sendeth rain on the just and on the unjust." Mathew 5:39-45*

Jesus lived by these same instructions. Everyone around him observed the ease with which he carried them out on every given situation. Scripture says, he was tempted in all things like us. "*…but we have one who has been tempted in every way, just as we are—yet he did not sin. Hebrews 4:15B.*

The burden he carried following these rules were far less than the burden of carrying grudges, bitterness and unforgiveness. Having lived these rules in plain view of his disciples, he knew they were ready to be taught to live by them. Initially, they might be hard to follow, but with faith and practice they can be done with ease.

****

Three

Struggling with Forgiveness

****

Like Peter of old, many of us living today are struggling with forgiving people that had sinned against us. You only have to talk to people around you to know how difficult they find it to forgive others. One day, I was talking to my friends in England coming back to the states from Sierra Leone. We were having some good conversations. We talked about a variety of things, and it drifted to the subject of forgiveness. I told a story of a minister whose son got killed by a thug. This minister happened to have a prison ministry, and he ministered in the jail of his son's killer. One day as he ministered, his son's killer accepted the

Lord and became born again. The story goes, this former thug now a Christian fell in love with the preacher's daughter, whose brother he had killed. The minister joined their hands in marriage. I then asked if there is any of us sitting that would have done likewise.

One by one my friends started saying what they'll do if they were in the preacher's shoes. Struggling to say how they will handle it. One of my friends had been quiet the whole time, so I ventured to get an answer from him. All the while he was slightly stooped. At my question, he straightened up and said with utmost seriousness, "I will kill him." My friend's reaction was natural and typical of humans. That is how people react when offended. We have a conscience of paying back. The "an eye for an eye" practice is still ingrained in us all.

Observed Occurrences

Unforgiveness had its place in every fabric of our world. In the home, the office, the church and every other institution that is governed by man. I have seen dispute amongst family members who were once tightly knitted and are now worst enemies. I have seen disputes amongst Church ministers. Great men of God who were once very close and worked together amicably, are now on none speaking terms. I have observed Christians, who are supposed to be the torch bearer, failed when it comes to forgiving their brothers and sisters in the Lord. I have seen good friends ended up being bitter enemies, all because one is not willing or able to forgive the wrong of the other. The interesting part is, people know that unforgiveness is the cause of their unhappiness. It is the cause of their anxieties and depressions at worst, yet they won't let it go. They'll rather carry that burden, enduring the unpleasantries instead of letting the matter go and live happily.

A good number of people know that God will not forgive their sins because they have not forgiven those that sinned against them. People understand that forgiveness is conditional; they know God's standard is unchangeable but still find it extremely difficult when it comes to forgiving others. Is it that people don't care to fear God? I think not. I think people hold on to these grievances because they don't know how to let it go practically. It occurred to me that there are a few reasons why it can be hard or almost impossible for people to forgive others.

I.   **Understanding The World We Live In.**

It is very evident that we live in a world that is full of wickedness. From the day sin entered the world the course of this world changed. That which should have been a beautiful world, a world of bliss, designed and crafted by the master builder, God himself, had gone horribly wrong. And that, by the finger of man. After creation, everything was beautiful and perfect; it was paradise on earth until the disobedience. God had commanded man not to eat of a particular tree and warned of the consequences if they do. Man disobeyed God's command and brought sin into the world. Sin then changed the whole dynamics of the world. Man was supposed to love and care for each other but instead began hating and killing one another. Man became wicked to the extent that God himself said, every imagination of man's thought was continually evil. *"And GOD saw that the wickedness of man was great in the earth, and that every imagination of the thoughts of his heart was only evil continually."* Genesis 6:5

When man was created, he knew one thing only, and that was to do right. Man had no knowledge of evil. There was perfect peace on earth. Adam and Eve had fellowship with God and were not afraid. However, all this changed when man became knowledgeable of evil and had since become an expert in doing evil to each other. This knowledge has been handed down from generation to generation.

Think for a moment of all the evil thoughts that are being executed by man on planet earth. Look at the news, see how people kill their fellow human beings. How people plan and scam other people off their hard-earned cash. How people are being trafficked as slaves even in this modern time. Sex and drug trafficking and all the other atrocities that man is engaged in. This is the world we live in. A world we are yet to understand fully.

II. The World from Man's Perspective

It is a proven fact that man understands the world differently. The evidence of wickedness is not denied because it is very present with us, man knows this is a wicked world. However, the irony is that man operates with an expectation that is parallel to this reality. Even though we know that wickedness is very present with us, we do not expect people to do wicked things to us. Because of this belief, we are unprepared for any wicked occurrence, and when they do happen, we react negatively. We desire to get even with the perpetrators. We become bitter and develop hatred, we get anxious and are stressed, simply because we are not prepared for such. This, in turn, influences our attitude, which affects the very many people we meet and interact with. These people then act in like manner towards us and other people they meet. It becomes a vicious circle that seems unbreakable. If we are to take a poll, we will hardly find someone who had prepared himself or herself in the event something bad is done to them. But that someone is aware that they live in a wicked world.

In sports meetings like soccer and the likes, fans and players alike, get into fights sometimes. Why? Because both teams had an unrealistic expectation. They both expect to win and that expectation will not turn out to be true for one of them. In any sports there are three outcomes, win, lose or a draw. But when the teams go to play, they expect to win and are therefore not prepared to lose. When they do, they react in negative ways.

In some neighborhoods, this expectation can be held so high that people are surprised when bad things happen around that area. A good friend of mine lives in a decent neighborhood so he thought it was all right to have left his car running on his driveway while he took a quick trip inside his house. When he came back, the car was gone. My friend knows he is living in a world where people steals but because he lives in this neighborhood, he did not expect it to happen to him. He was operating in this unrealistic expectation like everyone else.

Until man sees the world for what it is, and be prepared, there will always be a harmful and destructive reaction when reality kicks in. Unforgiveness is one such destructive reaction. Until man fully understands how the world operates, he will struggle to forgive others when they are wronged.

III. Classified People

In every generation, we hold certain people in high esteem. In our minds, we set moral boundaries within which we expect them to live. These are people like pastors, religious leaders, heads of states, or communities. Then we have our family members and friends, whom we hold to a slightly different but special standard as well.

People such as our family members are supposed to be loving and caring. They are categorized as people who will not hurt us at all. Doctors are supposed to be kind and morally upright and so must our pastors and bosses. We do not see these set of people falling below the moral compass we have set in our minds for them. Our interaction with them is based on that compass.

We fail to see them as everyday people with the potential to hurt us. And because we have these expectations of them, it hurts the most when they do hurt us. We feel betrayed and violated, and it becomes hard to even think of forgiving them. Of all people, they are the last sets of people we expect to do us harm. Almost all the time, incidents like these leave us perplexed and lost for words. Of all the people that could hurt us, we wonder why it should be our siblings or pastors or best friends. We can't comprehend why. The relationship that once was is now broken and that hurts. It hurts the most because we do not balance our expectations of people we esteem.

The fact is, we are humans with the potential to do wicked things, like everyone else regardless of how we are related. Regardless of our social or economic status. Until, we hold everyone to the same standard when it comes to human behaviors, we will be in for the shocks and surprises posed by such incidents.

Holding everyone to the same standard is not to make light or negate the standards of the high offices and their occupants. It is not to give a free pass to the people we esteem to do wrong because we deemed them regular people. Instead, it is for every one of us to be better prepared in case these people we esteemed hurt us. Generally, people have respect for each other and if we hold everyone with just that respect, it helps when we get hurt by anyone. There is no longer the esteemed category in our minds. Jesus once said these words to His disciples:
-

"Brother will betray brother to death, and a father his child; children will rebel against their parents and have them put to death." Mathew 10:21"

This is to show the depth of wickedness in the world and that all humans regardless of how we are related, can sin against us. Armed with such knowledge helps prepare the mind to absorb and deal with forgiving whomever it is that offends.

IV.   Man's Ego

Another area that enhances the struggle to forgive people is man's ego. The ego can be deceptive; it can either cause us to think more highly of ourselves or feel inferior to others. Those who think highly of themselves finds forgiving others very difficult. Such people have big egos. They walk with confidence believing in themselves, thinking they run the show. They get outraged when they are offended, their ego had been bruised and they will do what it takes to mend their bruised image. And forgiving the offender is not one of them, they will make sure the offender pays dearly. Teaching them and anyone else a lesson not to cross them or offend them in any way.

Contrary to people with big egos, we have people who have very low self-esteem. These are the people who see themselves inferior. These are probably more vulnerable than the people with big egos when it comes to forgiveness. A person with low self-esteem internalizes everything done to him or her. They don't have the ability to speak out on anything; they hold on to grudges and bitterness that stemmed from being wronged. They will hold on to these negatives regardless of how it is eating them up inside. They keep things inside till they can't hold it any longer and at that point, they will explode and vent out all the anger and other emotions they've held in for a long time. The momentary venting gives them a temporary satisfaction but they always sink back to that lonely place. Never able to even think of forgiving their offenders.

V. Understanding God's Sovereignty

If there is God, why all this suffering? Why all this injustice? How can he just sit there, seemingly doing nothing about the situations in the world? These are thoughts people ponder every day. They know and understand that God is good, powerful and mighty. People know God is just and he can do anything He chooses to and is answerable to no one. So why will this good God watch the thriving of wickedness? Why can't he just put an end to it? People just don't get it, and it baffles! This feeling or attitude of calling God to question or the inability to understand the way God operates is something from of old. Habakkuk, a prophet of God, was in a place at one time in history where he questions God. God was about to punish a nation that is less wicked by a more corrupt and vile nation. Habakkuk saw that as out of God's character, so he asked God why?

> *"How long, LORD, must I call for help, but you do not listen? Or cry out to you, "Violence!" but you do not save ³ Why do you make me look at injustice? Why do you tolerate wrongdoing? Destruction and violence are before me; there is strife, and conflict abounds. ⁴ Therefore the law is paralyzed, and justice never prevails. The wicked hem in the righteous, so that justice is perverted." Habakkuk 1:2-4*

In those words of the prophet, you can sense his frustrations, why can't God stop the madness? He knew that God is just, but he can't reconcile God's nature with what was going on at that time. Instead of executing judgement on the more ruthless nation, he is using them to punish one that is not that wicked. God was using Babylon to punish Israel, Why?

Another person that expressed the same sentiments as Habakkuk was John Baptist. John's primary mission was to introduce Jesus Christ to the world. He was an Old Testament prophet who declared that the reason he was preaching, was to reveal Christ the Messiah to the world. One day, as he was preaching he saw Jesus coming toward him.

John saw Jesus coming toward him and said, "Look, the Lamb of God, who takes away the sin of the world! "And I myself did not know him, but the one who sent me to baptize with water told me, 'The man on whom you see the Spirit come down and remain is the one who will baptize with the Holy Spirit. 'I have seen and I testify that this is God's Chosen One." John 1:29, 33-34

How exciting that must have been for John! He had revealed the savior, the righteous one, Jesus who was going to restore righteousness to Israel. All along, John's message had been one of judgment on the people of his days. He spoke of the ax at the root to strike down trees producing bad fruits.

> *"But when he saw many of the Pharisees and Sadducees coming to where he was baptizing, he said to them: "You brood of vipers! Who warned you to flee from the coming wrath? [8] Produce fruit in keeping with repentance. [9] And do not think you can say to yourselves, 'We have Abraham as our father.' I tell you that out of these stones God can raise up children for Abraham. [10] The ax is already at the root of the trees, and every tree that does not produce good fruit will be cut down and thrown into the fire." Mathew 3:7-10.*

John somehow believed that Jesus would execute judgment on the people but instead, Jesus was preaching salvation and healing the same people whom he was supposed to be judging. John got confused because Jesus was not doing what he had expected. He expected Jesus to judge the wickedness of the people in his days, especially when he, John was arrested and locked up and was eventually killed.

John the Baptist, was put in prison because he had preached against the King marrying his brother's wife. That was a righteous thing to do but he got locked up because of that. He had declared and believed in Jesus when he introduced him to Israel and the world. He believed Jesus would execute judgment on the evil doers but it turned out that Jesus was doing the opposite. In his confused state, he sent to ask Jesus if the world should expect another person to come. *"When John, who was in prison, heard about the deeds of the Messiah, he sent his disciples to ask him, 'Are you the one who is to come, or should we expect someone else?'" Mathew 11:3-4*

Jesus's response did not make it easy for him. Jesus responded: -

"Go back and report to John what you hear and see.⁵ The blind receive sight, the lame walk, those who have leprosy[b] are cleansed, the deaf hear, the dead are raised, and the good news is proclaimed to the poor. ⁶ Blessed is anyone who does not stumble on account of me." Matthew 11:5-6.

Jesus knew how John felt but he can't help it that he felt that way. Jesus said blessed is anyone who does not stumble because of him. This simply means that man must always throw down his ideas or thoughts when it comes to how God operates. No one knows what God's thoughts are unless he reveals them. In John's case, he thought it was Judgement time, but that was contrary from God's perspective.

I. God's Sovereignty Questioned Throughout the Ages

Throughout ages, men have been grappling the area of questioning God. Man had always kept an expectation of how things should work, we associate patterns with characters or personalities. When it comes to God, man has an expectation of how God will, or should do things. And when he does otherwise, it baffles us. Then the questioning and doubting begins. Since man can't figure God out, it is hard to understand him fully.

God is Sovereign, and he operates within his sovereignty. He does what is right by him and is answerable to no one. Many people, Christians and none Christians alike, have questioned God's ways. People have had questions like, why did God not start all over after Adam failed. People have and are still questioning why God, who is all knowing, gave us free will when he knows we will disobey him. Some are asking where is God with all this wickedness in the world. Why is he not doing anything to stop it? I can go on and on with these questions, and understandably so. We live in a world where terrible things happen to good people. A world where many things sometimes confuses us. Knowing that there is a God whom we know is good, all powerful and all loving. So, it is hard to reconcile his character with some of the things that are happening.

A. In Bible Times

In Bible times, there was a man called Job. The bible declared him upright and blameless in the sight of God. *"There was a man in the land of Uz whose name was Job, and that man was blameless and upright, and one that feared God and turned away from evil"* Job 1:1

At some point in his life, he suffered immensely. Job was a very wealthy family man who loved his wife and his kids. He had properties and cattle and flocks, but in one day, he lost almost everything. He lost all his children, his cattle and flocks and his fields all in what seems like seconds apart. Then not too long after that, he became very sick. He had boils all over his body. Now, this was a faithful man to God. His suffering stayed so long that Job's view of God was affected. He had this to say at some point about his anguish.

> *"Therefore I will not refrain my mouth; I will speak in the anguish of my spirit; I will complain in the bitterness of my soul. Am I a sea, or a whale, that thou settest a watch over me? When I say, My bed shall comfort me, my couch shall*

ease my complaints; Then *thou scarest me with dreams, and terrifiest me through visions: So that my soul chooseth strangling, and death rather than my life. I loathe it; I would not live alway: let me alone; for my days are vanity. What is man, that thou shouldest magnify him? and that thou shouldest set thine heart upon him? And that thou shouldest visit him every morning, and try him every moment? How long wilt thou not depart from me, nor let me alone till I swallow down my spittle? I have sinned; what shall I do unto thee, O thou preserver of men? why hast thou set me as a mark against thee, so that I am a burden to myself? And why dost thou not pardon my transgression, and take away my iniquity? for now shall I sleep in the dust; and thou shalt seek me in the morning, but I shall not be. Job 7:11-21*

The scripture vividly shows Job's frustration and anguish, maybe a little misunderstanding there as well. He was blaming everything on God. On his mind, there must have been a whole lot of confusion, is this really God? The one that I had known and had been serving all these years? Is he the same God? How come he is doing this to me? I can imagine Job's thought. Job had been serving God faithfully and had been doing his best not to sin against God and God indeed blessed him with a beautiful life. He was very wealthy and had a nice family. His commitment to God was outstanding. Bible declares him righteous but one day, his life changed, he had a very bitter experience, one that baffled him. Knowing that God is all powerful and just, he could not understand why such dreadful and horrible things happened to him. Especially, when he knew he had been walking uprightly with God. So, he questioned God. In situations like Job's we all do have some questions for God? We ask questions like why me? When things are going well for us, we are all good with God, but the moment things go a little awry the questions and doubts crawl in.

B. In Modern Times

Today, many of us do question God. It is as if he doesn't have rights to do certain things at all. We blame him for the conditions in which we find ourselves sometimes. We ask questions when a mishap occurs and we are even angry at God. Some of the struggles and sufferings we go through sometimes are by our own hands. Yet we blame and question God. He had given adequate instructions to live in the world but many of us had never once taken the time to read it. To know what he had said concerning the very thing that is making us sad and unhappy.

A principal human character is our ability to see and quickly reacts to the negatives, whilst taking the positives for granted. In a husband and wife relationship, a parent-children relationship, in a friendly relationship, we mostly see the terrible things done by the others in the relationship. We hardly complement the good deeds. That is the same attitude we have toward God. We question why God is letting wickedness continue. But if we are truly observant, we will be able to see God's greatness. His goodness and cares are displayed day in and day out. Look at the formation of the earth. The sun rises and the sun sets. The ocean has its borders. I can go on and on, consider the billions of people on earth and the food provisions. God is a good God. If only we train to look for the good things he had done, it will help us. One thing that stood out so boldly and is being trivialized by man, is this. God in his sovereignty, chose to send his Son to die for the sins of the world. This is the most blessings God bestowed on us. We are the guilty ones, God could kill us all and he will be right. Have you considered that? Until we have some sense of God's sovereignty we will struggle even as believers to comprehend and follow him with ease.

II.   God is Sovereign!

God is sovereign! This means, God has rights and within his rights, he can do as he pleases, and he is not obligated to answer to anyone. In his sovereignty, he chose to create the world and put man in charge of it. A beautiful place indeed with all that we need for survival. In his sovereignty, he explains how he operates differently than man. He said in scriptures, *"For my thoughts are not your thoughts, neither are your ways my ways, saith the LORD. For as the heavens are higher than the earth, so are my ways higher than your ways, and my thoughts than your thoughts."* Isaiah 55:8

The way God does things is different from how we do it. For us, a day starts in the morning but in the creation story, for each day, the Bible says, *"...And the evening and the morning were the first day."* Genesis 1:5b This phrase continues throughout the creation story for each of the six days. It seems God is counting a day differently than we do. We see it as morning and evening, but God counts it as evening and morning.

Another thing, we must know, understand and believe is, there are things that God kept secret from man. *"The secret things belong unto the LORD our God: but those things which are revealed belong unto us and to our children forever, that we may do all the words of this law."* Deuteronomy 29:29. One such secret is the way he does things. Because man is not privileged to these secrets, we reason God's actions. Trying to make sense of it from man's perspective and that always fails. Until man is comfortable with allowing God to be who he is, we will always have questions.

When God appears unto Moses, he sent him as his own servant to go free the Israelites from Egypt. Moses was afraid, he questioned, whom should I say send me? And God told him to tell them *"...I AM sent me..."* Genesis *3:13b*. In that one short phrase God laid it all out. He was telling Moses, I am he that creates the heavens and the earth. They belong to me. The seas and every created thing is mine and Moses, I can do with it as I please and I am answerable to no man.

In Job's case, God intends to let him know a little about his sovereignty and so he questioned Job.

> *Then the* LORD *spoke to Job out of the storm. He said:"Who is this that obscures my plans with words without knowledge? Brace yourself like a man; I will question you, and you shall answer me. "Where were you when I laid the earth's foundation? Tell me, if you understand. Who marked off its dimensions? Surely you know! Who stretched*

measuring line across it? On what were its footings set, or who laid its cornerstone— while the morning stars sang together and all the angels[a] shouted for joy? Job 38:1-7

Job could not answer any of God's questions, however, these questions that God asked Job brought him to the realization that God is indeed Sovereign! The only thing he could find to say back to God was affirming God's supremacy, God's sovereignty! Job said: -

Then Job replied to the LORD: "I know that you can do all things; no purpose of yours can be thwarted. You asked, 'Who is this that obscures my plans without knowledge?' Surely I spoke of things I did not understand, things too wonderful for me to know. You said, 'Listen now, and I will speak; I will question you, and you shall answer me. My ears had heard of you but now my eyes have seen you. Therefore I despise myself and repent in dust and ashes. Job 42:1-6

Here is one remarkable statement that Job made during his response, he said, my ears have heard of you but now I see you. In his dealings with God, there were attributes of God he had not come to understand yet. God's sovereignty was one of such, but after his experience with God, he understood that God is sovereign. He said, I repent and despise myself. So, he sat in dust and ashes showing his remorse for questioning the almighty God.

Hindrance to Forgiveness.

Another area that is worth talking about, is what I called the hindrance to forgiveness. Sometimes people in disputes can hold on to the illusion, that with time things will cool down, and the issue will be resolved. As appealing as this seems, there are a few problems with it. First and foremost, the idea is catering to people's inabilities, or their unwillingness to forgive the other party. The idea let the parties involved always go back to that illusion, without making any effort to take steps toward forgiving each other. Secondly, it is not guaranteed that it will happen all the time if at all it had happened before. The third problem with that is none of us knows what will happen the next minute, as it is not promised to anyone. What if either party of the dispute is no longer alive? And lastly, issues of the heart are not always resolved with time. If you can't do it now, it is likely you won't do it in a hundred years.

The second thing that is hindering forgiveness is self-condemnation. This mostly affects people who inflict or hurt others. Many people who had hurt others find it hard to forgive themselves. Maybe what they did was so gruesome, they can't see how that can be forgiven. And because they hold that view, they will not think about forgiving themselves.

I will remind us that we are flesh and blood and are therefore capable of doing any wicked thing. We must equally know that if we have felt sorry for what we did and had reached out to God and the people we did wrong, and had received their forgiveness, there should be no reason why we can't forgive ourselves. Holding on to self-condemnation brings anxieties, bitterness and self-hate which is equally deadly. It is an unhealthy way to live one's life.

****

Four

The Practicality of Forgiving Others.

****

Think of someone that had done you the most wicked thing on earth. Now imagine him or her in front of you, asking your forgiveness. You had just finished reading this book. You saw some points that make so much sense, and probably makes it looks a little easier to forgive. Now is the moment of truth. This person is now in front of you and you realize you don't have the strength or courage to forgive them. Memories of the incident come flooding your mind and you are incapacitated. Anger kicks in and your day turned sour. You realize that it is indeed hard to forgive.

Just because light has been shed on factors that cause one to struggle with forgiveness; (the world we live in man's expectations and God's sovereignty), means the real act of forgiving others is easy. These factors can help cultivate the spirit of forgiveness, but they do not make it any easier to forgive. The key to be able to forgive others is to learn to let God's will be done in our lives. This is not always easy, and the truth is God knows it is hard that is why he wants us to depend on him. Let go entirely and let God.

A perfect example was what Jesus did when he was in the garden of Gethsemane. The time of his crucifixion was getting closer and Jesus was feeling the pressure of it. He will be judged for the sins of the world. The world in general, Christian and none Christians alike, do not understand the devastation of sin. Jesus, the righteous, the man without sin, who had been in God's presence from the beginning, who understands sin and how it is shunned at by God, will take the sins of the world upon himself. The human side of him could not handle it, but he recognized God's authority, so he prayed, yielding to God's will. *"And he went a little farther, and fell on his face, and prayed, saying, O my Father, if it be possible, let this cup pass from me: nevertheless not as I will, but as you will."* Mathew 26:39

The humanity in Jesus was made visible and undeniable. His own wish then, was to let that cup of bitterness, that cup of disgrace, that cup of bearing the judgment of sin be passed from him. But he submitted to God's will. He said, not as I will, but as you will! When we as a people, we as Christians, get to that point when on each occasion, we yield like this, there will be nothing done to us that we can't forgive. Forgiveness will come like first nature.

Consequences of Unforgiveness.

Forgiving others is not like walking on a treadmill or doing pushups. Especially when someone in your inner circles is the perpetrator. By inner circle, I mean family members, such as husbands, wives, parents or children. By people that are esteemed like pastors, teachers, coaches and the likes. If you had experienced this type of hurt, you know it is the most painful, not only because what was done hurts, but more so because of the person that did it. It bruised the very core of one's being. The deed itself is only the beginning of a life-long pain and suffering unless you deal with it. It becomes a recurring pain that intensifies each time you think about it. You wake up on a beautiful morning, everything seems right and boom, that thought finds its way into your mind and changes your mood. Your mood, in turn, affects the people with whom you mingle. This generates bad relationships in your workplace and amongst your friends. The world will become a smaller place for you. Your trust in humanity is diminishing if it has not all gone. You develop anxieties, and on and on.

The consequences of holding grudges for offenders by anyone is grave. This offender is controlling your life! He seemingly has power over you, even though he is not there physically. Is this something you really want to subject yourself to? This person, might not be even thinking about you, but you are bored down with thoughts about him or her. Not sure how much people know that we live our thoughts. Bible says as a man thinks, so he is. If you let the thought of the hurt someone did to you, take control of your mind, yours is a sad life to live. You will be tormented day in and day out by someone else, who might not even have you in their minds.

Some of you have been hurt terribly in the past and you are still holding on to it. And because of that, your life is not what it should be. You see others enjoying themselves but you can't. Even the few times that you've ventured made no difference. The hurts keep coming back and takes away your joy each time. You just can't seem to be able to let it go. It is indeed hard to live your life like that.

In situations like that, people's minds get locked down in a circle. Hopelessness and other by-products of unforgiveness becomes a pattern, and it seems difficult to break free. Our minds are shut down to the good things that beckons to us daily. One such thing I would like to point out is the fact that you survived whatever it is that was done to you. Think about that, God, in His mercy did not let whoever hurt you, kill you.

People who hold on to unforgiveness are suffering unnecessary pains, live unpleasant and hopeless lives, and if such a person stays in that state till death, they will not be forgiven by God. Think about that. Now, this offender, whoever he or she might be, have not only troubled you in time, but now in eternity as well. God's word is clear, you will not be forgiven if you do not forgive your offenders! Look at what was done to Jesus who is our Lord and Savior! Do you think, you have been done more wrong than what was done to him?

In Forgiveness, the Buck Stops with God.

Sometimes people take consolation in the idea that God will punish the people who had offended them someday soon. They will hold onto these offenses in their hearts anticipating God's judgement on their offenders. What they fail to understand is that their offenders have the same access to God as any of us do. Scripture says, *"for God so loved the world…" John 3:16.* So, if the person that offends you at some point in their lives, realizes that they need God's mercy and accepts Christ and asks God's forgiveness, that person will die and go to heaven. While you will miss heaven because you did not forgive. When it comes to forgiveness, the buck stops with God.

All sin that man commits is against God. Be it murder, adultery or whatever the sin, it is primarily against God and he is the only one whose forgiveness counts. If you sin against man, (which is a sin against God) and asks and get his forgiveness, it doesn't mean God have forgiven you. It does not make you less guilty before God. If you do not ask God's forgiveness, your sin stays. But if you ask God's forgiveness and let's say the other person is not within reach for you to ask his forgiveness, you are forgiven by God.

King David understood this principle very well. He used it after he sinned against Bathsheba and Uriah. When he went before God to pray for forgiveness after committing adultery and murder he prayed "*Against thee,*

thee only, *have I sinned, and done this evil in thy sight: that thou mightest be justified when thou speakest, and be clear when thou judgest. Psalm 51:4*

Notice the choice of words David used. He said he had sinned against God and God only had he sinned against. In that prayer David was not making light of the fact that he did sin against Uriah, Bathsheba and their relatives. He was not ignoring what they went through. He was not denying that he had hurt others by his actions at all. David was simply stating that when it comes to sin, it is only God who forgives!!! Scripture says *If someone sins against another person, God can mediate for the guilty party. But if someone sins against the LORD, who can intercede?" 1st Samuel 2:25.* Think about that!

The thief that was crucified alongside Jesus is another example. The thief had sinned against a good number of people in his days. He was a thief by profession, so he stole from anyone whom he could steal from. He probably killed a few people along the way. He was being put to death because of his crimes against humanity, but he knew to turn to the Lord and asked for his mercy. The moment he did, the Lord pardoned him and he is in paradise now. He did not have a chance to go look for the guys he had robbed. He did not ask for anyone's forgiveness, he only asked the Lord to remember him when he (the Lord) come into his kingdom.

> *But the other answering rebuked him, saying, Dost not thou fear God, seeing thou art in the same condemnation?* [41] *And we indeed justly; for we receive the due reward of our deeds: but this man hath done nothing amiss.* [42] *And he said unto Jesus, Lord, remember me when thou comest into thy kingdom.* [43] *And Jesus said unto him, Verily I say unto thee, Today shalt thou be with me in paradise. Luke 23:40-43*

The Lord took him in that day! That is God's way of doing things. That man had been wicked all his life and had seemingly received a free pass from God. Truth is God loves every one of us and had sent out an invitation to all. Those who respond will get the benefits and those who don't will miss out. In Ezekiel, the Lord declares His ownership of man. *"Behold, all souls are mine; ....: the soul that sinneth, it shall die." Ezekiel 18:4.* In this one verse, God laid down the principle by which he judges. He said the soul that sins, dies. Continuing that verse, God told the Israelites this:-

> *"But if the wicked will turn from all his sins that he hath committed, and keep all my statutes, and do that which is lawful and right, he shall surely live, he shall not die. All his transgressions that he hath committed, they shall not be mentioned unto him: in his righteousness that he hath done he shall live.*

What the thief did was simply a shift from unrighteousness to righteousness as prescribed by God. He believed in Jesus the savior of the world. His sins were forgiven end of story. God is the ultimate forgiver of sins.

Reconciliation Formula

Letting go of people's wrong is hard and I understand that. I have had my fair share of trials. I was hurt terribly in my early Christian years by someone that was in my inner circle, my former pastor. A man with whom I bonded. We used to be such friends, a man that was instrumental in my growth as a Christian and was an encouragement to my ministry.

I was in college and had a fiancée whom I had intentions of marrying. One weekend, I came home from the Bible school campus, and she told me something inappropriate transpired between them. I listened to her story and went back to campus for classes without telling anyone.

That week, when the pastor came to the school to lecture, I pulled him to the side and told him what my then-fiancée had told me about them and then asked if that was true. That question spiraled into a long painful and bitter experience for me. What he did hurts so bad I had to tell him I can't forgive him at that moment. I told him I'll have to pray for God's strength to do so. I felt what it meant to be under bondage. I understand what it meant to be carried away by your thoughts. I suffered the brunt of holding a grudge. I spent hours thinking of him and what he did. I prayed and prayed and eventually was able to forgive him. After doing so I was relieved of the pains and hurts I once had. I was able to sit in his car again and talked freely when chanced. So, I do understand how people feel when they get hurt by anyone, especially a loved one.

I must say, it was also an opportunity for me to grow because, not only did I know what it feels like to be relieved of my misery, it also let me see humans as humans. Prior, to that incident, I saw the pastor as a perfect man whom I should follow at any cost, it was as if I was worshipping him. I had to repent and ask God's forgiveness for that and thank God for his goodness and faithfulness, he forgave me.

The Lord understands the pain we go through when we are hurt by someone. He lived it, he endured it and had set an example for us by which we too can overcome. He knows that we will get hurt or will hurt someone else even as Christians. It was with this knowledge that he laid down the principle for us to keep unity and peace in the body. He prescribed a method with which we can reconcile with each other in times of conflict.

While Christians should not go around anticipating conflicts from one another, we should be very much cognizant of the fact that conflict is very possible. So, when we encounter one we have the Lord's prescription to follow.

Moreover, if thy brother shall trespass against thee, go and tell him his fault between thee and him alone: if he shall hear thee, thou hast gained thy brother. But if he will not hear thee, then take with thee one or two more, that in the mouth of two or three witnesses every word may be established. And if he shall neglect to hear them, tell it unto the church: but if he neglect to hear the church, let him be unto thee as an heathen man and a publican. Mathew 18:15-17

When you understand the scriptures, you will know that one of its theme is unity. God intends for us to be a unified body. He wishes all mankind should get along well. The unfortunate side is we live in this world where wickedness seems to be prevailing. So, to make the best out of the situation in this world, humanity should be able to forgive and reconcile. The whole teaching of forgiveness is to get people united.

One thing I will like to point out while we are on the reconciliation topic is the Lord has not put us under bondage. He made it clear that reconciliation is between two people and not just one person. If someone doesn't want to reconcile we don't have to force them. The scripture gives clear-cut steps to take when a brother or a sister offends you. If you take all these steps and the other brother or sister refuses to reconcile, you can't force him or her. You would have done your part. Leave such brother or sister alone but be sure not to harbor any grudge for him or her. Remember the scripture says, as much as it depends on you, live in peace with all men. If someone doesn't want to be at peace with you let it be, only be sure to have a clear conscience before God. And at whatever time a brother or a sister come to reconciled you should be ready.

It is ironic that many of us Christians are familiar with the verses in *(Mathew 18:15-17 quoted above)*, but they only come alive when we preach or teach them. They only come alive when we are in the congregation listening as it is being preached or being taught. But when it is time to practicalize these very scriptures, we toss them out of our minds. We've been hurt terribly and therefore, it is not a good time for the scriptures. It is time to take revenge on others that had hurt us.

In the church, God's home, where his children live and worships; you hear of factions. A set of brothers and sisters ganging up against another set. A sister is not on speaking terms with another sister. You hear of ministers not talking to each other. You hear of fighting within the church. Sometimes we keep smiling faces pretending we are at peace to all, but deep within we hold on to grudges and un-forgiveness toward another brother or sister. I have seen with my own eyes, Christians in conflict. I've always looked at such incidents as opportunities for us to step up and reflect God's love. But each time as I have seen it, they've failed to do so. Picture for one moment, a believer in the Lord that had been wronged, forgives and publicly embraces his offender. Extending the right arm of fellowship again. What a sight that will be.

In my heart, I believe that God our Father had always been longing for the day when one of his children will endure his brother or sister. When it doesn't matter, what was done to brother "A," but he let it go because of the love of God in his heart. I believe that God is longing to see a brother reach out to another who had hurt him and win them over again! God's desire for his children is unity and love. No earthly father love seeing their children in a fight. If earthly father's desires that for their children, what do you think God our Father desires? God wants to see his children loving each other. He wants us to understand the world we live in. He wants us to be able to cultivate the attitude of forgiving one another, and so draw people that are yet to know the Lord even closer.

In his letter to the believers of his days, Peter said this: *"And if the righteous scarcely be saved where shall the ungodly and sinners appear." 1 Peter 1:18.* Peter had observed the attitude of Christians in his life time. Christians are to be like Christ but on many occasions, they acted contrary just like we do today. So, Peter was exhorting them to be more mindful of how they live. If we who are Christians, who have been renewed in our minds, who have the Holy Spirit indwelling us. If we can find it hard to forgive, what will the unbelievers do? We as believers have got to step up, so through us, those who are yet to believe will see a reason to believe also. When we do so, we will be displaying the Christ like attitude befitting Christians.

Benefits of Forgiveness.

Forgiveness has its benefits when it is exercised. It benefits both the forgiver and the forgiven. On the part of those who forgive, weights are lifted off their shoulders. There are no more countless hours of brooding over what someone did to them. These hurtful thoughts no longer ruined their moments and days. They are being relieved of those burdens. They can now interact with the offenders in meaningful ways, possibly working their way to refined relationships. Anxieties are gone and their trust in people, society and the world at large are built up again.

On the other hand, those who receive forgiveness are grateful in more than one ways. Firstly, they feel relieved that they had been forgiven. It feels like getting a doctor's report that one is cancer free after some time battling the deadly disease. They will develop confidence again to interact with the offended. Forgiveness is all about reconciliation. Imagine a husband being forgiven after he had cheated on his wife or vice versa. Imagine what it means for the children. What a reunion that will be. It saves kids from growing up with emotional inconsistencies that might come to play later in their lives. Forgiveness ends the vicious circle of hate and wickedness.

The Bible records an interesting narrative of two brothers, who displayed forgiveness in practical terms. Jacob and Esau were twin brothers born to Isaac and Rebekah. They grew up in a seemingly divided home. Isaac loved Esau and Rebekah loved Jacob. Isaac, their father intended to bless Esau.

When he was old and getting close to his death, he asked Esau to prepare him a meal so that he can eat and then bless him. It so happened that Rebekah overheard when Isaac asked Esau for the meal. Rebekah quickly arranged with Jacob and together deceived Isaac. Rebekah prepared a meal, dressed Jacob in Esau's clothes and cover his hands with animal skin so that he feels like Esau. Esau was a hairy man.

"And it came to pass, that when Isaac was old, and his eyes were dim, so that he could not see, he called Esau his eldest son, and said unto him, my son: and he said unto him, Behold, here am I. And he said, Behold now, I am old, I know not the day of my death: Now therefore take, I pray thee, thy weapons, thy quiver and thy bow, and go out to the field, and take me some venison; And make me savoury meat, such as I love, and bring it to me, that I may eat; that my soul may bless thee before I die. And Rebekah heard when Isaac spake to Esau his son. And Esau went to the field to hunt for venison, and to bring it. And Rebekah spake unto Jacob her son, saying, Behold, I heard thy father speak unto Esau thy brother, saying, Bring me venison, and make me savoury meat, that I may eat, and bless thee before the LORD before my death. Now therefore, my son, obey my voice according to that which I command thee. Go now to the flock, and fetch me from thence two good kids of the goats; and I will make them savoury meat for thy father, such as he loveth: And thou shalt bring it to thy father, that he may eat, and that he may bless thee before his death. And thou shalt bring it to thy father, that he may eat, and that he may bless thee before his death. *11 And Jacob said to Rebekah his mother, Behold, Esau my brother is a hairy man, and I am a smooth man: 12 My father peradventure will feel me, and I shall seem to him as a deceiver; and I shall bring a curse upon me, and not a blessing. 13 And his mother said unto him, Upon me be thy curse, my son: only obey my voice, and go fetch me them. 14 And he went, and fetched, and brought them to his mother: and his mother made savoury meat, such as his father loved. 15 And Rebekah took goodly raiment of her eldest son Esau, which were with her in the house, and put them upon Jacob her younger son: 16 And she put the skins of the kids of the goats upon his hands, and upon the smooth of his neck: 17 And she gave the savoury meat and the bread, which she had prepared, into the hand of her son Jacob. 18 And he came unto his father, and said, My father: and he said, Here am I; who art thou, my son? 19 And Jacob said unto his father, I am Esau thy first born; I have done according as thou badest me: arise, I pray thee, sit and eat of my venison, that thy soul may bless me. Genesis 27:10-19*

Jacob pretended to be Esau brought the soup Rebekah had prepared for Isaac, their father. He ate and blessed him. As soon as he had blessed Jacob, Esau walked into his father's room with the soup. Isaac then perceived Jacob had deceived him. He told Esau Jacob had tricked him and got the blessings meant for him. Upon hearing that Esau vowed to kill Jacob. His hatred for him grew beyond imagination. Jacob had taken Esau's birthright over some stew earlier, and now had stolen the blessings he coveted. *"And Esau hated Jacob because of the blessing wherewith his father blessed him: and Esau said in his heart, the days of mourning for my father are at hand; then will I slay my brother Jacob." Genesis 27:41*

Rebekah their mother became aware of Esau's plan and sent Jacob away for fear that Esau will kill him. So, they were separated since, and had no clue of each other's whereabout. Both men grew up in their separate ways and became successful. But Jacob, it seems had not forgotten what he did to his brother. Sometime later, he sought to reconcile with his brother Esau. He sent messengers to go and appeal to Esau in a bid to appease him before they met.

> *"And Jacob sent messengers before him to Esau his brother unto the land of Seir, the country of Edom. ⁴ And he commanded them, saying, Thus shall ye speak unto my lord Esau; Thy servant Jacob saith thus, I have sojourned with Laban, and stayed there until now: ⁵ And I have oxen, and asses, flocks, and menservants, and womenservants: and I have sent to tell my lord, that I may find grace in thy sight.*
> Genesis 32:3-5

Their reconciliation was classic. Scripture says, Esau ran up to his brother Jacob, fell on his neck and kissed him. It is recorded that they wept in an embrace.

> *And Jacob lifted up his eyes, and looked, and, behold, Esau came… And Esau ran to meet him, and embraced him, and fell on his neck, and kissed him: and they wept. Genesis 33:1a&4*

What a joyous reunion and a display of forgiveness. Esau did not take into consideration the hurt Jacob did to him, he embraced him. What a sight! Prior to their meeting, Jacob and his household were fearful of Esau. Because Jacob had displayed his fear of Esau to his wives and children. Think of how relieved they all were at this point. Esau's act of forgiveness halted what might have been a vicious circle of hate. They were rejoicing. All the hurts and fears have been put to rest. At this instant, the families were united because Esau forgave Jacob.

****

Five

Living with the offender after forgiveness.

****

After forgiving someone, how do we live and interact with them again? When someone hurts us, betrays our trust, it is hard to live with them again. However, doing so can forge a stronger relationship that is stronger than it was before the betrayal. This is not always easy but when it is done, it is beneficial. The question is how can we live together again after a betrayal? How can we work ourselves to that place of trust again? Trust is vital to any relationship. Looking into the scriptures, I found a formula God uses regarding residing with the reconciled.

"For I will forgive their wickedness and will remember their sins no more." Hebrews 8:12

He forgets our sins. When we sin, it hurts God, and it affects the relationship between a loving God and his people.

Time after time God gets angry and punishes the people He loves because of sin. As a loving Father, He really does not take pleasure in disciplining his children. But because he is holy, he does not overlook sin. So, when we come to him asking for his forgiveness, he forgives and forgets our sins.

Forgetting something is like it never existed. Think about the times you have forgotten something. That thing is gone from your memory. It had been erased, removed from its placeholder in your mind and you do not think about it anymore. So, when God forgets the sins he has forgiven, there is nothing against us. It is as if we had done nothing wrong, and that enables Him to love us again. What a brilliant formula!

Adopting this formula will enable us to forget the sins of the people we have forgiven. God said, *"I will…remember their sins no more…"* God is deliberate, he chose to forget the sins he forgives. If we are to adopt this formula, we should be deliberate in forgetting these offenses committed against us. Because remembering the hurtful things can bring us back to a place of anger and bitterness, stirring up un-forgiveness within us.

Understanding God's formula is one thing, the next is how to implement it? How do we go about forgetting offenses done to us? We can do so by conditioning our minds, because we all live our thoughts. What we think, is what translates to our actions and forms our characters. Paul the Apostle, knew that too well. He used that principle when admonished the believers in Rome in Bible times. Paul was talking to them about living the new life after they had been converted to Christianity from a life of sin. He wrote,

"Likewise reckon ye also yourselves to be dead indeed unto sin, but alive unto God through Jesus Christ our Lord." Romans 6:11

Paul was telling them to reckon "(be of the opinion)" that they are dead to sin. This means even though the possibility for them to sin is real, their mindset should be "they are dead to sin." With that mindset, it is easy to triumph over temptation when they arise, keeping them from sinning.

Deducing from this same scripture we should be of-the-opinion-that we have forgotten the hurts and wrongs of all whom we have forgiven. This will not come overnight but if we constantly put it to practice, we will be able to do just that. One thing we must understand is, if we forget these sins of others, we can live and interact with them like we use to be before they hurt us.

In his letter to the Philippians, Paul the Apostle wrote that they should forget the things of the past. For Paul to be as successful of a gospel minister as he was, he had a lot to forget. The beatings he received, the threats and hates from the religious leaders, the imprisonments he endured. Just to count a few of his encounters. He was able to forgive them all because he said: "*…but I focus on* *this one thing: Forgetting the past and looking forward to what lies ahead…" Philippians 3:13.* In the book of Isaiah, the Bible admonished us to forget the former things and not to dwell on the past. The wrongs done to you are in the past and if you forget the past, you will forget the incident and so the hurt will not surface anymore.

After Reconciliation

There is a beautiful story of forgiving and forgetting the wrongs of others recorded in the Bible. Not only did this scripture shows us life after reconciliation, it also shows how forgiveness plays a huge role in God's plan. Joseph, the eleventh son of Jacob was betrayed by his brothers and sold into slavery. In that betrayal, God had a plan that was fulfilled because Joseph not only forgave his brothers but was able to live peaceably after their reconciliation.

God's Plan Accomplished Through Forgiveness

God has a plan for every one of us. He had called each of us and had assigned tasks to us. When he spoke to the prophet Jeremiah, He told him: -

"Before I formed thee in the belly I knew thee; and before thou camest forth out of the womb I sanctified thee, and I ordained thee a prophet unto the nations." Jeremiah 1:5

As God knew, formed and ordained Jeremiah, so had he done to every single one of us. Before we were formed, he knew us and had scheduled a task for each of us to do while on Earth, and these tasks are for the benefit of the whole. The truth is, some of us will find that calling and obey and others will be too busy doing their own thing.

Since creation, man had been God's way of accomplishing his will and purpose on earth. Sometimes, the road to achieve God's purpose can be a rough ride.

Joseph, who was sold by his brothers had one such rough ride in his life. Like every other man, Joseph did not know how his life will play out. He was just living as regularly as he can in his days when his life took a dramatic turn. Being who he was, he took every moment gracefully and would later reveal that it was God's plan for his life.

"But now, do not therefore be grieved or angry with yourselves because you sold me here; for God sent me before you to preserve life." Genesis 50:20

Those were the words Joseph said to his brothers who sold him when he was only a boy, at their reconciliation years later. He realized that despite his brothers' wicked acts toward him, God had a plan, and that plan, was paramount. His brothers had sold him into slavery, but he later told them that God hath sent him there so that he can save lives.

This all began when Joseph was a young child. He was living with father Jacob, his two wives and eleven brothers. The bible says that Jacob, their father loved him very much, and that love was displayed in front of his brothers daily. Their father gave him a coat that had significance to it.

"Now Israel loved Joseph more than all his children, because he was the son of his old age: and he made him a coat of many colors. And when his brethren saw that their father

loved him more than all his brethren, they hated him, and could not speak peaceably unto him." Gen. 37:3-4

This display of love by their father, made the rest of his brothers angry and they began to harbor hate towards Joseph.

Jacob was a herd's man whose children, except for Joseph and their youngest brother normally took the cattle out to feed. On one fateful day, Jacob sent Joseph to go see how his brothers were doing in the fields with the cattle and Joseph was excited to go.

One day, Jacob sent Joseph to go to see his brothers in the field where they were watching their flock. Joseph was excited to go see them and took the trip. When his brothers saw him, they quickly plotted amongst themselves to kill him.

"And when they saw him afar off, even before he came near unto them, they conspired against him to slay him. And they said one to another, Behold, this dreamer cometh. Come now therefore, and let us slay him, and cast him into some pit,

and we will say, some evil beast hath devoured him: and we shall see what will become of his dreams." Genesis 37:18-20.

While Joseph was happy to go see his brothers, they quickly plotted to kill him when they saw him coming toward them. Had it not been for their eldest brother, they would have killed him. Eventually, they did not kill him but was sold into slavery. Imagine what Joseph was thinking at that time. The fact that, his brothers sold him. The fact that his status had instantly changed. He was now a slave from the cherished and favored young son of his father. He looked at his own brothers as they took the money and sent him to servitude.

God's plan in the making.

The people that bought Joseph were merchant and they also sold him to an Egyptian officer called Potiphar. This man, Potiphar quickly realized that his house was being blessed because of Joseph. He set Joseph in charge of his house and all his possessions and Joseph was at his peak again. Not that he preferred that position to the comfort he had with his family, but compared to be one of the servants, his promotion was a comfortable place to be. At this point, Potiphar's wife had set eyes on him and wanted to sleep with him. She had been tempting him every chance she had, but Joseph kept turning her down.

> *"And after a while his master's wife took notice of Joseph and said, "Come to bed with me!" But he refused. "With me in charge," he told her, "my master does not concern himself with anything in the house; everything he owns he has entrusted to my care. No one is greater in this house than I am. My master has withheld nothing from me except you, because you are his wife. How then could I do such a wicked thing and sin against God?" Genesis 39:7-9.*

One day the bible story continues, Joseph came into the house and the wife was there by herself. She quickly grabbed him wanting him to sleep with her. Joseph ran out of the house and left his cloak with her.

Armed with Joseph's cloak, she told everyone that Joseph came into the house to molest her. Joseph was sent to jail right away. I would imagine his thoughts as he was transported. Once again from a comfortable life to a life of hardship. Joseph, like any of us, would have thought of his brothers' wicked acts many times.

God's plan unfolded.

In prison, Joseph found favor in the eyes of the Jailor because the hand of God was upon him. He was made an overseer of all the other prisoners. At some point, two of the King's workers were thrown in jail, they met with Joseph and forged a friendship. One day, when Joseph came to see them, he noticed they were not quite their usual selves. He inquired and learned that they both had dreamt the night before. Joseph interpreted their dreams and true to his words, the interpretations were right. The butler was restored to his place in Pharaoh's palace but the baker was killed per Joseph's interpretation. Joseph then pleaded with the butler to remind Pharaoh of his fate when he was released but the butler forgot all about him once he was out.

One day, Pharaoh had a dream he could not understand and was looking for someone to interpret the dream. It was then that the butler remembered and testified of Joseph to the King. Joseph interpreted the King's dream and this led to his coronation as the second in command in Egypt. He was then put in charge of the conservation and distribution of the foods. Not long after, according to Pharaoh's dream, famine hits the entire world. Egypt had plenty of food stored up for this exact moment in the world's history. They had that much food because Joseph interpreted Pharaoh's dream.

Pharaoh had dreamt a period of acute famine in the world but prior to these years, there will be years of bountiful harvest. Joseph was put in charge of managing the harvest in the years of plenty. He kept enough food stored up to feed the people for many years.

When the famine started, word spread all over the world that Egypt has plenty of food and so people from everywhere were coming to buy.

One day, as people were pouring into Egypt to buy food, Joseph's brothers came along also. Those who conspired to kill him. Those brothers, who tore off his coat, that beautiful coat their father made for him. Those brothers who sold him to slavery, betrayed his trust in humanity. They came to buy food. They came to buy from none other than Joseph! Their own brother whom they had betrayed. They did not recognize him but Joseph recognized them. Imagine the emotions that went through Joseph at that time. He had every opportunity to take revenge on them. He had the authority, the ability, and above all, the reason to be vengeful toward them. But instead, he felt sorry for them.

One day, Joseph revealed himself to his brothers and they were dumbfounded, and very terrified. They couldn't hold his gaze. Joseph had to intreat them to relax and that he meant no harm.

"Then Joseph said to his brothers, 'I am Joseph; does my father still live?' But his brothers could not answer him, for they were dismayed in his presence. And Joseph said to his brothers, 'Please come near to me.' So they came near. Then he said: 'I am Joseph your brother, whom you sold into Egypt. But now, do not therefore be grieved or angry with yourselves because you sold me here; for God sent me before you to preserve life." Genesis 49:3-5

Joseph forgave his brothers and in doing so, God's plan to save lives through Joseph was fulfilled. He was sent ahead to Egypt to prepare for the famine that would have killed thousands of people. Joseph was in God's perfect plan for his life. He followed through, endured the betrayal, the mistreatment, the lies, he endured them all. Over and above all, he forgave it all. Because of Joseph's attitude toward his brothers, God's plan for his life manifested. A whole nation called Israel was formed. And from Israel, the entire world was blessed.

Imagine if Joseph had taken matters into his own hands. He had rights to be angry at his siblings, and now that he had power, he could have had his revenge. Maybe kill them or throw them in jail forever as they did to him. Had he done that, it is very possible that it might have hindered God's plan to build the nation of Israel.

Generally, people believe God can do anything he wants to do regardless of man's response. History had taught us that after the first six days of this earth, God had been using man to accomplish his purpose on earth. So, it is possible for man to hinder God's plan. Adam, the first man did when he disobeyed God's command. Like Adam, when we fail to do what God called us to do, we may very well be hindering God's plan on earth. Failing to forgive might very well be a big contributor to hinder God's plans for people's lives. Don't let that be!

My Thoughts

Forgiveness is hard, maybe one of the hardest crosses we have been called to bear. But it can be one of the best things that can happen to us equally. Let us examine the facts once more. Because we live in this world, we will encounter hurts. People will hurt us.

Dealing with these hurts regardless of their magnitude depends mostly on our understanding of the art of forgiveness. Those of us who understands it, know that if we hold on to the offenses that are done to us, our lives will be miserable. We will be filled with malice, bitterness and hatred. And we will poison our immediate and extended environment. Remember attitude goes a long way. There never will be a right attitude with grievances within.

If you let go of the wrongs done to you, you are not missing anything at all. After all, who wants to be sad, bitter and unhappy? Who wants to be depressed and be pitied? These are the types of things people who hold on to grudges get. When you let go of these wrongs, you will be free from the unnecessary burdens that goes with unforgiveness.

You will bring happiness to people, put smiles on their faces. You will be an inspiration to others. You will even help those who offend you to be better. Above all else, you will be in right standing with God in that regards.

Living with the offender after forgiveness

Remember, God sent Jesus to be the example for us. Terrible things were done to him, but he forgave it all.

This calls for work on each of our part. It is not easy to forgive as had been emphasized throughout the pages of this book but remember the benefits it brings to you when you do. So, each of us should set our minds to live a life of forgiveness. Here is how that works, the Bible says: -

> *"Do not repay anyone evil for evil. Be careful to do what is right in the eyes of everyone.* **18** *If it is possible, as far as it depends on you, live at peace with everyone. Romans 12:17-18.*

In these two verses of scripture, lies the whole method of how to live in peace. Note that the emphasis is on "you!" It is not common for people to refrain from retaliating on those that offends them. The Bible is saying to you and I that we must refrain from doing that. If we all go out and live our lives like this before long, we will revolutionize the world. The world is in dear need of peace.

Man had been trying in our own little ways to foster peace in the world but have failed in almost all instances. There are organizations like the UN, the OAU, and the likes. Their biddings and intentions are all good. They want to foster peace in the world; but achieving their goals had always been a challenge because, the disputed parties are not willing to let the other party go. They are not that forgiving and so they get stalemates most of the times in peace talks amongst nations.

We have been called to do what these prominent organizations can't do, we've been called to foster peace. We are ambassadors of peace if we will live according to the quoted verses above. God is counting on us, remember God has a plan for the world, and he had called everyone who will obey to help execute that plan. Are you willing? Are you in God's plan? If so, let's remake the world one soul at a time. Live in peace with all men! The God of peace strengthened you all through and through Amen. Forgive all who had hurt or offend you now that you know. God bless you!

Living with the offender after forgiveness

www.ingramcontent.com/pod-product-compliance
Lightning Source LLC
LaVergne TN
LVHW051504070426
835507LV00022B/2925